CRAFT YOUR
STASH

Transforming Craft Closet Treasures into Gifts, Home Décor & More

LISA FULMER

Design Originals

an Imprint of Fox Chapel Publishing
www.d-originals.com

About the Author

Lisa Fulmer

Lisa Fulmer is an artist, crafter, designer, writer, and marketeer. She strives to bring creativity to all of her work, whether she's drawing and painting for herself, designing projects for craft industry manufacturers, managing blogging and social media efforts for clients, or consulting with businesses about their marketing plans. Lisa also writes a weekly column called *Creative Space* for her town's popular local news blog. Her designs have been published in magazines and compilation books, and her work can be seen on many popular community craft sites. Visit Lisa at *lisalizalou.com*.

ACQUISITION EDITOR: Peg Couch
COPY EDITOR: Laura Taylor
COVER DESIGNER: Ashley Millhouse
LAYOUT DESIGNER: Kerry Handle
PAGE DESIGNER: Lindsay Hess
PROJECT PHOTOGRAPHY: Scott Kriner
EDITOR: Katie Weeber

Acknowledgments

My heartfelt thanks go out to:

My online craft community at large, whose support and inspiring work keep me in a constant state of delight.

The craft industry designers—my amazing colleagues who are global catalysts for creativity.

My crafty confidants—Andrea, Angela, and Glenna—glitter-and-glue-doused besties who kept me laughing and motivated while making this book.

My friend and mentor Tiffany, who helped me grow my career in this industry.

My friends and family who knew me B.C. (before crafting) and still love me despite my endless blathering on about paints and papers and such.

My mother, who painted beautiful canvases; my father, who crafted treasured woodwork; my godparents, who made lovely jewelry; and my grandmother, who sewed her heart out—you each instilled in me a deep appreciation of all things creative, for which I am very grateful.

ISBN 978-1-57421-873-2

Library of Congress Cataloging-in-Publication Data

Fulmer, Lisa.
  Craft your stash : transforming craft closet treasures into gifts, home décor & more / Lisa Fulmer.
     pages cm
  Includes index.
  ISBN 978-1-57421-873-2
  1. Handicraft. 2. Recycled products. I. Title.

TT157.F85 2014
745.5--dc23

2014014996

© 2014 by Lisa Fulmer and New Design Originals Corporation, *www.d-originals.com*, an imprint of Fox Chapel Publishing, 800-457-9112, 1970 Broad Street, East Petersburg, PA 17520.

Special thanks to Choly Knight for the color wheel illustrations appearing on pages 18, 20, and 21.

Printed in China
First printing

Introduction

If you're like me, you love, I mean really LOVE, to shop for craft supplies! You (and I) rarely buy things because you've run out, though. You buy things because they're pretty or new, or because you saw a cool demo for a product you'd like to try, or you got to meet a designer and you'd like to replicate her work, or maybe there was a coupon just burning a hole in your pocket.

You slowly, but surely, fill up every one of your closets, shelves, drawers, and tote bins with oodles and oodles of arty crafty goodness: this is your *stash*.

You adore each and every stash you have. You like to look at it, rearrange it, ponder over it, and brag about it. Paper, fabric, stamps, stickers, buttons, bling, die-cuts...you love it all!

If this sounds familiar, then this book is for you. It's all about taking stock of your stash and giving you some creative options to make some little dents in it.

I've designed lots of stash-worthy projects that I think you and yours will really enjoy using or giving as gifts. They're suitable for any skill level and can be customized to fit your personal style. I've also included some organizing tips, my favorite and indispensable craft tools, and lots of great techniques.

Each project is designed for you to dig into your stash and customize the materials to make it yours. You can either follow my design or go rogue, baby!

I want to help you enjoy the second half of that shopper's high. You have your stash, now let's craft with it!

Lisa Nemer

CONTENTS

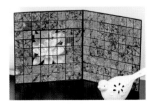

TOOLS AND TECHNIQUES

Before you get started, let's take a look at some of the tools and supplies you'll need to make these projects. We'll also cover some tips and techniques for working with paints, brushes, stamps, and adhesives.

⸙ ABOUT METRIC ⸙

Throughout this book, you'll notice that every measurement is accompanied by a metric equivalent. Inches and feet are rounded off to the nearest half or whole centimeter unless precision is necessary (note that some larger measurements are rounded off to the nearest meter). Please be aware that while this book will show 1 yard = 100 centimeters, the actual conversion is 1 yard = 90 centimeters, a difference of about 3 15/16" (10cm). Using these conversions, you will always have a little bit of extra yarn if measuring using the metric system.

Stash Essentials

I consider these tools and supplies to be the essentials for every crafter's pantry...like sugar and flour or salt and pepper. There are lots of other gadgets and materials to think about buying when a particular project calls for them, but these basics will carry you through plenty of good crafting!

Surfaces
- Patterned and solid papers
- Cardstock and chipboard
- Wool felt
- Patterned and solid cotton fabrics
- Wood panels and plaques
- Foam sheets, balls, and blocks

Cutting, punching, and measuring

- 8" (20.5cm) scissors
- 4" (10cm) scissors
- Nonstick scissors
- Fabric shears
- Handheld rotary cutter
- 12" (30.5cm) rotary paper trimmer
- Metal ruler
- Wide acrylic ruler
- Craft knife
- Wire cutters
- Small and large self-healing cutting mats
- Punches in a few basic shapes (square, circle, star)
- Round corner punch
- Photo corner punch
- Regular ⅛" (0.5cm) hole punch
- Heavy-duty ¼" (0.5cm) hole punch

General tools

- Craft drill
- Flat-nose beading pliers
- Round-nose beading pliers
- Heat gun
- Bone folder
- Stencils

Paints, inks, and mediums

- Rubber or acrylic stamps
- Clear and color permanent stamp pad inks
- Acrylic paints and inks
- Alcohol inks
- Gloss or matte medium
- Découpage medium
- Fine-point and chisel-tip permanent markers
- Colored pencils
- Small and large paintbrushes
- Foam brushes and wedges
- Palette knife
- Scrapers (notched and straight edge)
- Nonstick craft mat or parchment paper
- Wood skewers, toothpicks, and craft sticks
- Baby wipes, cotton swabs
- Mister bottles, plastic cups

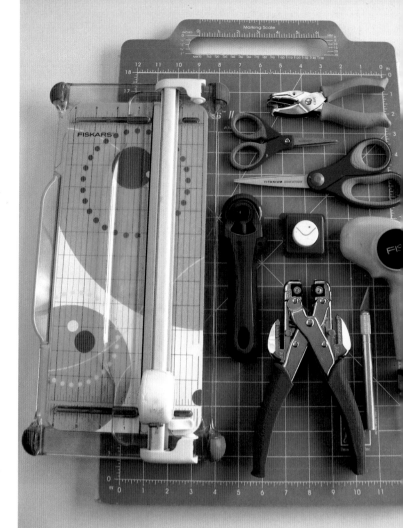

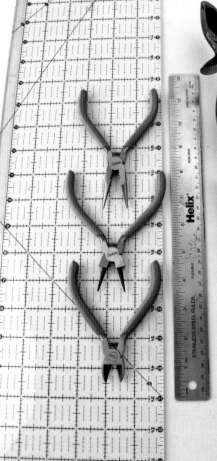

Techniques

Here are some of my favorite techniques that I use all the time—I hope you'll find something new to try!

Acrylic paints, inks, and mediums

Craft or "student" quality paints are less expensive and fine for general use. "Artist" quality paints are more expensive with deeper, more brilliant pigments. Acrylic paints, inks, and mediums can be blended with water or with each other to create custom colors and consistencies.

Acrylic inks are quite versatile. Use them straight with a brush or dip pen for bold coloring or staining on any porous surface, such as paper, fabric, or wood. A few drops will tint clear mediums or water mist sprays. Thin inks with a little water to paint watercolor effects.

Acrylic paints are fun to blend. Use equal amounts of two light or medium colors to create a third color that will complement them both, or use a small amount of white or dark gray to make colors lighter or darker. Blend paints with a fluid medium to minimize brushstrokes, cover large surface areas faster, and keep paints wet and workable on your palette longer. Blend paints

Adhesives

- White tacky glue
- Permanent bonding adhesive
- Heavy-duty glue stick
- Hot glue gun and glue sticks
- Small and large glue dots
- Dimensional glue dots or double-sided adhesive foam squares
- Paper-backed, double-sided tape
- Tape runner
- Painter's tape

Embellishing

- Stickers
- Rub-ons
- Flat-back gems and rhinestones
- Metal and plastic charms
- Buttons
- Beads and findings
- Ribbons and embroidery floss
- Twines and wires
- Paper or silk flowers and leaves
- Fine and coarse glitters

Artist quality acrylic paint (left) produces richer, more brilliant hues than most acrylic craft paints (right).

with texture or gel mediums when you want to add thickness and dimension to your painting. Fabric medium blended with paint will prevent the fabric from getting too stiff as you paint on it. Thin acrylic paints with water to create tints, gradients, and water washes.

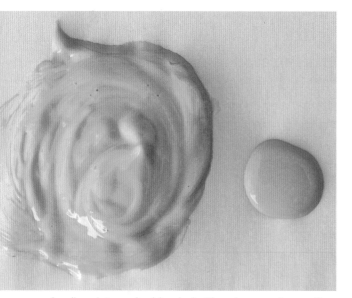

Acrylic paints can be blended with various mediums with little or no loss of color. This matte medium has been blended with acrylic craft paint at a ratio of twelve-to-one.

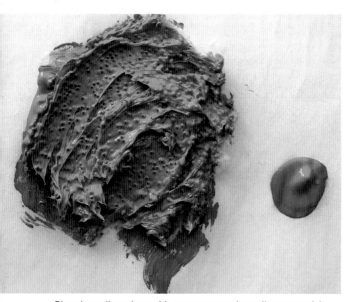

Blend acrylic paints with texture or gel mediums to add thickness and dimension to your painting.

Brushes

Paintbrushes come in a wide range of shapes and sizes that can vary significantly between brands. Just choose the brush that works best for the application and the coverage you need—foam or bristle, thin or thick, flat or round, narrow or wide. More expensive brushes are generally very well constructed and more durable, but standard brushes can last a long time with proper care.

Always keep a container of water and paper towels handy when painting. When you're finished painting, wipe the excess paint on a paper towel, then place the brush in the water until you're ready to clean it. While acrylic paints are water based and nontoxic, it's the better environmental choice to allow most of your leftover paint to dry first and then throw it in the garbage rather than wash it all down the drain.

Using a flat piece of parchment paper or a nonstick craft sheet as a palette makes it easy to scrape large amounts of excess paint back into airtight containers when you're done with a project. Keep some cardstock, wood, canvas, or cotton fabric on hand for wiping leftover paint from your brushes and you'll have your next project started!

Paintbrushes last longer if you don't use them to stir or blend paint. Use skewers, toothpicks, craft sticks, or a palette knife instead. Avoid going past the heel of the brush when you're dipping it into a jar of paint to prevent paint from caking where the bristles or foam are secured to the handle.

Save old and stiff brushes for dry-brush techniques, and keep a dry cosmetic powder brush handy for sweeping away excess glitter on projects.

Stamps and pads

There are rubber stamps and acrylic stamps, each with their own set of pros and cons. In general, rubber stamps can be carved more deeply to provide a crisper, more detailed impression. Acrylic stamps are popular because you can see through them to the object you're stamping, they're less expensive, and they take up less storage space. Foam stamps are available in bold, solid shapes that are great for stamping with paint. All stamps can be cleaned with alcohol-free baby wipes or a little soap and water.

Many stampers enjoy collecting stamps of themed or detailed illustrations to make greeting cards and other paper crafts. Images can be stamped in a single color using an inkpad or in multiple colors using special markers. Stamped areas can be embossed with heat-reactive powders or colored in with pencils, pens, and watercolor techniques.

I'm not a traditional stamper myself, but I love using my stamps and inkpads in all kinds of nontraditional ways! I gravitate toward smaller, basic images that are great for creating surface designs on fabric and debossed impressions on foam or clay. I also love the large, singular patterns for creating interesting background textures on paper or wood, and sentiment stamps are fun for adding words to artist trading cards and art journal pages.

The stamp's partner in crime, the inkpad, can live a very full life without ever being touched by a stamp. An inkpad can be used like a brush to swipe color on the edges or across the surfaces of your project. Dab a cosmetic sponge applicator or a stiff brush on the pad to smudge a little color anywhere you like. There are different types of ink for pads—most are either dye-based or pigment-based. Dye ink dries more quickly than pigment ink and works well on a variety of surfaces; pigment ink is more colorfast than dye ink and works best on porous surfaces. There are lots of different formulations for each type of ink that impact permanence or allow you to create special effects.

Adhesives

Ahhh, the sticky stuff...it quite literally holds everything together. People often tell me they are confused by all the different kinds of glues and tapes on the market and don't know what to use on which project. The two main things to consider when choosing an adhesive are the types of surfaces you're adhering and the overall durability needed for the project. Beyond that, it boils down to personal choice between brands, prices, availability, odor, and the type of applicator bottle or tube it comes in.

In general, dry adhesives like double-sided tape, tape runner, and glue dots work best with paper-to-paper projects. When using liquid glues in paper crafting, it can be a bit tricky to keep the paper from getting too wet and curling or buckling, plus sometimes the glue lines can show through the paper. But if you need better adhesion from edge to edge than you can get with a dry adhesive, paint on a very thin coat of plain white glue or découpage medium with a brush. For larger surface areas, try a glue stick.

A tacky white glue is great for adhering heavyweight porous surfaces like cardboard, foam, felt, botanicals, or wood. If you want to speed up the drying time, try using a hot glue gun instead of a liquid glue (but you have to work quickly!). Use a permanent bonding adhesive for nonporous surfaces and for heavier items that need to hold up against gravity. There are specialty glues formulated for specific surfaces like fabric, stone, vinyl, or glass, some of which I have found give better results than the everyday glues.

I don't think you need to run out and buy a different glue for every project, though. Start with a basic glue designed for either porous or nonporous surfaces and see how it works. If your project doesn't feel strong enough when the glue is dry, then go check out a specialty glue. Don't forget the hardware stores...they often have a wide selection.

ORGANIZING YOUR STASH

As crafters, we all tend to go a little overboard on supplies and we love to buy what's new or pretty.

If we don't have some kind of dedicated storage space to keep our stash organized, though, we are bound to buy more of what we don't need or already have. I can't tell you how many times I was sure I had a certain type of ribbon or cardstock or brads, but I couldn't find them when I needed them. So off to the store I went, only to find the items later when I got home with my new purchases.

Now don't get me wrong, I am all about shopping for new craft supplies—online and at my local craft stores, hardware stores, or secondhand stores. But because my stash is organized, I can avoid buying more of what I already have and instead spend my craft dollars on trying something new.

Call me obsessive, but I'm a big fan of the old adage "a place for everything and everything in its place." I also regularly fall prey to the "out of sight, out of mind" syndrome, so organization is pretty important to me. I really believe that no matter if you're crafting in a spare room, the bedroom, the garage, or on the kitchen table, you will be more inspired and more likely to enjoy the process of creating if your supplies are organized. Then when you can't find what you need for a particular project, you'll know it's because you don't have it rather than because it's totally buried and you'll have to spend lots of time looking for it. Organization not only helps prevent you from buying more than you need, it also helps you find what you need in your existing stash.

Now I haven't always been organized, and I don't always practice everything I preach. I often work from home, and crafting is part of my job, so for the past several years I have lived in a house with an extra bedroom that I turned into a studio office. I thought more space would surely make it easier to stay organized. But alas no...before I really invested some time (and a little money) into my storage solutions, my supplies were either piling up on my work table, spilling over into the hall closets, or they remained inside unopened bags on the floor...and then before too long, my workspace started encroaching upon the living room sofa and kitchen table. This "dreaded spread" *will* happen without organization, no matter if you craft in a dedicated room or in the corner of the family room.

For me, nothing kills my creative mojo faster than tons of clutter. It can put me deep into shopping moratorium mode: "I'm not buying one more thing!" We've all been there, right? But when that happens, you might miss out on the opportunity to really enjoy trying something new.

Some people don't mind clutter and can still find inspiration to create in the middle of it, and that's cool. But if you're like me, you feel the need to clean up and clear away the remnants of earlier projects before you can feel open and ready to start new projects.

Next time you're sitting in the middle of a cluttered pile of craft supplies, consider this question: How does disorganization affect my creativity?

Storage solutions for any space

Here are just a few storage ideas from my own studio that will work for just about any space, small or large.

Get in the zone. Whether you're organizing a drawer, a cupboard, a closet, or a whole room, it helps to divide the area into zones to keep similar types of supplies together. Make zones for tools, fabric, paper, small embellishments, paints, glues, markers, stickers, etc. That way, when you aren't sure whether or not you have a particular item, you only have to search for it in one zone, which saves so much time!

Magnetic spice jars. These are perfect for buttons, flowers, charms, brads, or any small embellishment. Display them on a magnetic white board along with your favorite notes and pictures. With the clear lids, it's easy to see exactly what's inside each one.

Labeled paper drawers. Categorize your papers by color or pattern type and label stackable drawer sets to match. Stack them into a tower on the floor or line them up along a countertop or shelf. I bought these four-drawer portable cabinets at a quilt show; they were intended for storing 12" (30.5cm) quilt blocks in progress, but they work great for all my scrapbook papers.

Fabric storage bins. I love using these little bins to store small in-progress projects or items I just bought that I plan to use in the near future. Using open bins for things that would otherwise clutter up my workspace gives me more freedom to move back and forth between projects without completely putting them away, plus they're easy to travel with when I need a project to work on with my craft groups. Fabric bins are also very handy spots to tuck away new purchases until I decide where to store them.

Rolling kitchen island. This is one of the best investments I've made for my studio. A countertop at standing height makes a very flexible workspace. It has drawers and cupboards for storage, as well as a paper towel holder and bars for hanging rulers and templates. It's easy to

MAGNETIC SPICE JARS

LABELED PAPER DRAWERS

FABRIC STORAGE BINS

ROLLING KITCHEN ISLAND

PRINTER STAND

move around on wheels—I put it in the center of the room to access a project from all sides, but I also slide it against the wall when I need floor space or move it closer to the window when I want natural light.

Printer stand. A tall printer stand with adjustable shelves works well in small spaces. It's perfect for storing bins and baskets, as well as holding larger tools and gadgets like die-cutting machines. Because it's open on both sides, I placed it perpendicular to the wall in a narrow space between my desk and the doorway.

Open wire cabinets. Not only do the tops of these cabinets give me extra workspace, the deep drawers hold loads of fabric. I can see what colors are where, and each drawer is easy to pull out and place on the floor, bed, or table to sort through to find what I need.

Silverware trays. These make great organizers for pens, pencils, and markers. I can easily pull one out of a drawer to take with me wherever I feel like sitting to draw or doodle.

OPEN WIRE CABINETS

SILVERWARE TRAYS

CUPCAKE DISPLAY STAND

FOOD CANISTERS

Cupcake display stand. With a mini custard cup in each spot, this stand is both adorable and useful for keeping lots of different little embellishments close at hand.

Locker shelves. These folding wire racks make it easy to take advantage of typically unused space way up high on a closet shelf. They're tall enough to rise above most books and magazines, giving you an out-of-the-way spot to stash the stuff you don't use very often.

Food canisters. I love these semi-clear plastic containers for sugar and flour. They're rectangular, so they fit nicely on a shelf side by side, and I can see exactly what's inside.

Squat mason jars. First of all, they're just plain cute! Second, they're perfect for storing embellishments, buttons, clips, and other small items. I glued a circle of foam core to the bottom of each jar so they can nest together in a stack.

LOCKER SHELVES

SQUAT MASON JARS

CD/DVD shelf unit. I took the doors off the closet in my studio and lined the interior walls with a couple of CD/DVD racks. They have lots of adjustable shelves, and because they're so shallow, I can see all of my supplies at a glance.

Foam cylinders. I love saving bits of ribbon from gifts, packaging, or the ends of rolls to use on greeting cards. But they were becoming an unruly cluster in a basket, and I couldn't tell what I had. Now they're neatly wrapped and pinned to smooth foam cylinders that I hung between chains.

Wall-mounted drawer shelves. A shelf and drawer in one! Who doesn't love a good two-fer?

These drawers are super shallow, but they fit my rubber stamps like a dream!

Cupboard labels. I love all the storage space in the cupboards beneath my counters, but it's easy to forget what's behind closed doors. Plus I hate having to get down on the ground to dig around, trying to remember what I put way in the back. So I put self-adhesive plastic business card sleeves from the office supply store inside each cupboard door. I can easily read the list and quickly pull it out of the sleeve to update it as needed.

CD/DVD SHELF UNIT

FOAM CYLINDERS

WALL-MOUNTED DRAWER SHELVES

COPY PAPER
NOTE PADS
CARDSTOCK
ENVELOPES

PAPER TOWELS
VINYL ROLLS
INTERFACING

XMAS CARDS

CUPBOARD LABELS

DESIGN BASICS

There are lots of great books about the principles and elements of design for all different forms of creative work; I highly recommend reading as many as you can! Learning more about design can help you improve your skills; it gives you tools to build more confidence and helps you recognize when it makes more sense to save it or scrap it. Understanding design makes it easier to work through those miserable, yet inevitable, "craft fails" we all experience. They say that every mistake is a design opportunity, and I believe it!

In this chapter, I want to outline just a few design basics as they relate to crafting. If you haven't delved into any design books yet, you'll at least get a little taste of what goes into good design here, and hopefully you'll feel more comfortable about going rogue with craft projects to make them your own.

But I'm not here to enforce any rules—I'm actually all about breaking the rules when it comes to creative expression. What's most important to me is that you enjoy the *process* of creating—don't fret too much about the results you get. As Ernest Hemingway said, "It's good to have an end to journey toward; but it's the journey that matters, in the end."

Color

A crafter's best friend might just be the color wheel, especially when you're creating with colors you might not personally wear or decorate with. How color impacts design can be somewhat subjective, as we all have our favorite colors and our not-so-favorites. There is much to learn from the theories behind color, from how it's physically perceived, to how it symbolizes seasons and experiences, to the way it evokes emotion and influences behavior.

Color wheel

life is about
creating yourself

I believe!

just be exactly who you are

Primary colors

Cool

Warm

Warm and cool colors

Secondary colors

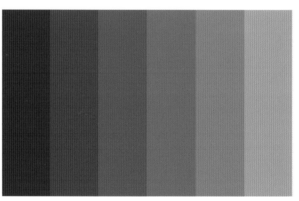

Add white to any color to create a lighter shade

Tertiary colors

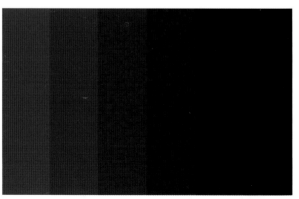

Add black to any color to create a darker shade

Color theory begins with three categories of colors: primary, secondary, and tertiary. The three primary colors are red, yellow, and blue. Mixing two primary colors produces the secondary colors orange, green, and purple. When you mix primary and secondary colors, you can produce six tertiary colors, like blue-green or yellow-green. This information is very helpful for blending paints. You can literally create any color you want just by using the three primary colors, and you can adjust the shade any way you want by adding white or black.

Achieving color harmony makes any ho-hum craft project look so much better, no matter what materials you're working with and no matter what style or genre the project is. Harmony means the mix of colors is both unified and engaging, but not too blah and not too crazy—you achieve a perfect balance!

Nature gives us all kinds of color harmony—photos of plants, trees, and flowers are wonderful tools for choosing colors for a project. You can also be successful by keeping warm tones together or cool tones together. Add white to a color to create a matching gradient of tints that grow progressively lighter, or add black to create a collection of darker shades.

A 12-part color wheel also gives you some easy formulas to create harmony.

- Analogous color scheme: any three colors that are side-by-side on the color wheel
- Complementary color scheme: any two colors that are directly opposite each other on the color wheel
- Split complementary color scheme: a combination of three colors, using one color plus the two colors adjacent to its complement
- Triadic color scheme: any three colors or shades that are evenly spaced around the color wheel

Analogous color scheme

Complementary color scheme

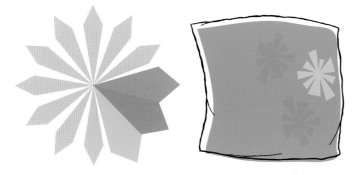

Split complementary color scheme

Triadic color scheme

Balance

Balance means the elements of your design are arranged in a way that looks pleasing and puts the focus where you want it. Balance can be symmetrical (formal and safe) or asymmetrical (casual and dynamic), as long as there is an equal distribution of weight from one side to the other.

You can create balance horizontally, vertically, and/or in a radiating, circular kind of way, like the spokes of a wheel or numbers on a clock face. Take a look at the examples below and on page 23 to see how balance was achieved in each one.

This pillow has a symmetrical, horizontal design paint-stamped on the fabric. Even though the scraps of fabric below the trees were randomly sewn together, I placed the buttons evenly to make the stripe look more balanced.

I combined small, square, stamped images in a circular, symmetrical pattern, alternating the more delicate flower print evenly with the bolder stripes, like a quilt block.

The diamonds in this fabric greeting card repeat identical patterns across the top half and across the bottom half.

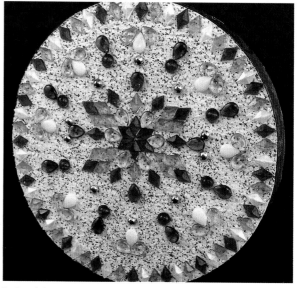

I glued these small gems in a radiating format to make this Christmas ornament, taking advantage of the variety of pointed and curved shapes to create interesting repeating patterns.

You can make or break balance with your choices of colors, textures, shapes, and placement. Good balance is really important in scrapbooking and card making, for example, so your focal point is noticed and supported, but not overshadowed, by your embellishments. The "rule of three" is always good to remember, too. Objects arranged in groups of three (as well as other odd numbers) are inherently more engaging and harmonious.

This black and white wall hanging is an asymmetrical assemblage of paper and fabric with metallic accents. The focal point, the large flower in the top left, is balanced by a similar floral design in the bottom right of the diagonal hillside. The butterflies and trees are grouped in threes, which gives them motion, forcing your eye to travel around the groupings.

⤐ **TIP** ⤏

Have any of the projects on pages 22–25 struck you as the perfect craft to try? Get full instructions for making them at *lisalizalou.com*.

This square scrapbook layout is vertically asymmetrical. It looks balanced in part because pink and green are complementary colors (they are opposite each other on the color wheel), and also because I placed a triangular arrangement of embellishments around the photo, with larger elements on the left to counter the weight of the frame on the right. The patterned green paper is flat, and the holographic-style pink plastic is shiny, but in spite of their surface contrast, their patterns share a similar texture. I also raised some of the elements up off the page to give it more dimension.

Texture

For me, texture is everything in crafting. There is such a huge variety of dimensional textures—embossed paper, soft fabric, smooth buttons and charms, sharp bling, rough wood, and fuzzy yarn.

Texture can also be less tactile and more visual—think repeating patterns, lettering, or layered colors. Many papers have printed patterns to mimic textures like brush strokes, woven fabric, stone, stucco, etc.

Contrasting textures often work well together in a project, like metal accents on fabric, silk ribbon on cardstock, or sparkly beads on wool. Texture can become too overpowering really fast, though. You'll want to use it in a way that creates extra interest without compromising the overall unity of your project.

Check out the photos on this page and the next and see how the different textures stand out in each one. Consider how you can add texture to your craft projects.

BOX LID: Sand texture medium, metal, ink-marbleized acrylic, chipboard.

GREETING CARD: Torn handmade paper, foil-embossed medallion, resin charm, nonwoven polyester.

WALL HANGING: Embossed foil, wire, and metal charms on wood.

POSTCARD: Chunky glitter, sheer ribbon, plaster charm, netting, fabric tag.

WALL HANGING: Nonwoven polyester, glass bead medium, stiff interfacing, Angelina fibers.

GREETING CARD: Painted and scratched acrylic, printed texture paper, resin charm.

WALL HANGING: Sand texture medium, melted nonwoven polyester, crinkled foil, sandpaper, metal charm.

GREETING CARD: Sponge dauber inks, high-gloss medium, glass bead medium, mica flakes.

Unity

Unity in design is a bit challenging and nuanced. It happens when all the various design elements and principles are effectively integrated together to create an overall look that is really powerful. When you see a project that instantly grabs you—you just fall in love with it right there on the spot—it's probably because of unity. You aren't necessarily even seeing all the cool individual parts of the design at first. Instead you're responding to how it all works in concert to make a broader statement that you can personally relate to. As Aristotle said, "The whole is greater than the sum of its parts."

PROJECTS

Now that you have all your supplies organized and you've learned a few techniques and design tips, it's time to start crafting! Each project is designed to encourage you to dig into one of your stashes. The majority of the projects call for basic tools with beginner-friendly construction. Remember—I'm all about breaking the rules, cutting corners, and going rogue! Have fun altering my designs with your own favorite materials and colors to make them your own.

Happy

u +
me

Mom & dad
1960

You make life wonderful

INSPIRE
3197

Personal Calling Cards

✿ **STASH ITEMS: Cardstock, flat-back gems**

A personal calling card is not just a heartfelt ode to eighteenth-century etiquette; it can also be an artistic expression of your personality.

A business card can sometimes be too stuffy (or maybe you don't want to give out your work information). But there are lots of occasions when you might want to share your personal contact info, your blog address, a book you recommend, or even your favorite quote, and calling cards are perfect for that.

Personal calling cards are easy to whip up ten at a time. They're perfect for setting up play dates for the kids, meetings at the dog park, or some sweet, old-fashioned courtship. Hey, it's better than writing on a cocktail napkin or the palm of your hand!

SUPPLIES
* Heavy, letter-size, solid color cardstock
* Rubber stamp
* Inkpad and matching fine-point marker
* Chisel-tip marker (optional)
* Paper trimmer
* Pencil and ruler
* Flat-back gems
* Embroidery floss
* Clear gel craft glue

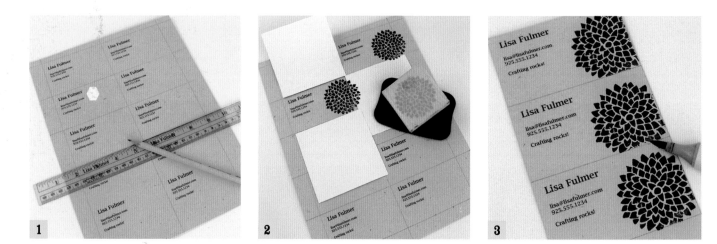

1   **Measure and mark the cards.** Use a ruler and pencil to measure and lightly mark off a sheet of cardstock into 2" x 3½" (5 x 9cm) sections (the size of a typical business card). If you aren't thrilled with your own penmanship, you can set up a template in a word processing or graphics program on your computer to print out your information first.

2   **Stamp the cards.** Pick an inkpad color that coordinates or contrasts with the color of your cardstock. I love gold and purple together. Stamp your favorite image (I love dahlias, too!) on the side of each card. To stamp off the edge of each card, use large sticky notes to cover the surrounding cards as you stamp.

3   **Fill in the stamps as needed.** It can take a little practice to get just the right amount of ink and pressure when you stamp. Fill in any lighter areas as desired with a matching marker.

Personal Calling Cards *(continued)*

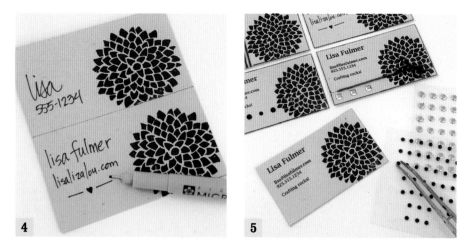

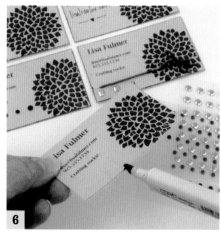

4

5

6

4 **Add lettering.** If you like a more casual look, have fun adding lettering to each card with a fine-point marker.

5 **Trim and embellish.** After the ink is completely dry, trim out each card just inside the pencil lines. Embellish each card by gluing on flat-back gems and/or wrapping them with embroidery floss.

6 **Ink the edges.** If desired, ink the edges of the cards with a chisel-tip marker for a crisper finish.

TIPS

Look for cardstock that is solid on the front and patterned on the back.

Try stamping your image to create a vertical card instead of horizontal.

Decorate some "blanks" to carry with you and write in your name and details as needed for a specific conversation.

Mosaic Scrapbook Layout

STASH: Paper scraps

We can't bear to toss out even the smallest scraps from our best scrapbook papers, right? I like punching shapes out of the smaller pieces as I go and storing them for later use. My favorite punch is the 1½" (4cm) square—it's perfect for making paper mosaics with random bits of pretty patterns and colors.

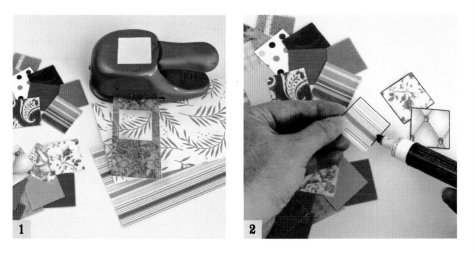

SUPPLIES

* ❊ 12" x 12" (30.5 x 30.5cm) sheet of black cardstock
* ❊ Paper scraps in a mixture of colors and patterns
* ❊ Solid color cardstock
* ❊ Personal photo
* ❊ 1" or 1½" (2.5 or 4cm) square paper punch
* ❊ Decorative photo corner punch
* ❊ Tape runner
* ❊ Black chisel-tip marker
* ❊ Sentiment stickers
* ❊ Journal tag or sticker
* ❊ Self-adhesive gems
* ❊ Clear ruler

1 **Punch the squares.** Punch 50 to 60 squares from the scraps of paper. Select colors and patterns that coordinate or contrast nicely with each other.

2 **Ink the edges.** Ink the edges of each square with the black chisel-tip marker. Covering all the white edges of the paper squares will make the colors pop off the black background.

u + me

mom & dad
1960

You make life wonderful

xo
ox

Mosaic Scrapbook Layout *(continued)*

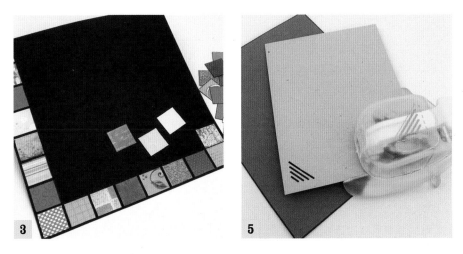

3 **Lay out the squares.** Place the squares on top of the black cardstock, evenly distributing them in a grid pattern with about ⅛" (0.5cm) of space between each square. Leave space in the lower right corner of the cardstock for a photo frame and a smaller space to the left of the frame for a journal tag.

4 **Adhere the squares.** After you've arranged a mosaic pattern that you like, adhere each square to the cardstock with the tape runner. Use a clear ruler to keep your rows and columns straight and even if necessary.

5 **Create the photo frame.** Trim two pieces of solid color cardstock (I used green and gold) to create a double-mat frame for your photo. Punch the corners of the inside frame with the photo corner punch, and ink the edges of the outside frame with the black marker. Adhere the frame in position on the cardstock.

6 **Finish and embellish.** Adhere the journal tag in place and embellish the layout with sentiment stickers and self-adhesive gems. Slide your photo into the frame and write a caption on the journal tag.

❧ TIPS ❧

Be aware of papers that have pops of bold color or those with similar patterns or shades—space them out to balance your mosaic and give it a random, yet cohesive, look.

A group of mosaic layouts in an album makes a nice gift for a busy parent. Add generic or seasonal sentiments and leave the frames empty for the recipient to add her own photos.

Change the papers and colors in your mosaic layout to enhance the style or theme of the photo (yes, it's okay to punch squares out of full sheets...I promise not to call the paper police!).

Shaker Card

❀ **STASH ITEMS: Recycled packaging, seed beads**

Greeting cards are so much more fun with a little shake, rattle, and roll! Save the plastic packaging from your charms, tags, brads, and other craft store purchases—those little clear raised windows are perfect for trapping seed beads or glitter. Sometimes I even buy embellishments just for the packaging (like I need an excuse to buy more embellishments, right?). The plastic I used for this card came from a package of metal circular sentiment charms. I promise I will find a way to use the charms...someday.

SUPPLIES
* ❋ Cardstock in several solid colors
* ❋ Patterned scrapbook paper
* ❋ Plastic packaging window
* ❋ Double-sided, paper-lined tape
* ❋ Glue dots
* ❋ Seed beads
* ❋ Flat-back gems
* ❋ Sentiment charm
* ❋ Paper trimmer
* ❋ Scissors
* ❋ Craft knife
* ❋ Cutting mat
* ❋ Metal ruler
* ❋ Pencil
* ❋ Bone folder

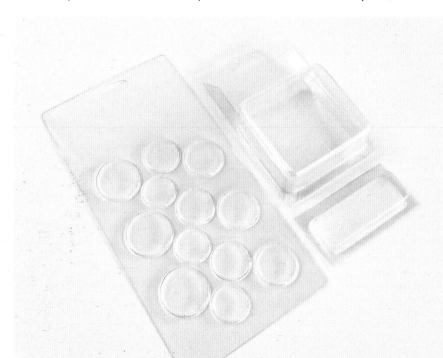

Plastic packaging makes clever windows for the front of greeting cards or other projects.

1 **Prepare the card.** Trim the base cardstock to 7" x 10" (18 x 25.5cm). Score and fold the cardstock in half to 5" x 7" (12.5 x 18cm). Trim the scrapbook paper to 4¾" x 6¾" (12 x 17cm), and adhere it to the center of the front of the card with double-sided tape.

2 **Prepare the window.** Cut the plastic packaging so there's at least a ¼" (0.5cm) flat border surrounding the raised window area.

3 **Cut the frames.** Choose two colors of cardstock to make a double-mat frame for the plastic window. Trim the cardstock for the bottom frame ½" (1.5cm) larger on all sides than your plastic window. Trim the cardstock for the top frame ¼" (0.5cm) larger on all sides than your plastic window.

1

Shaker Card *(continued)*

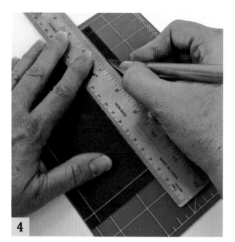

TIP

Trap glitter inside a small square plastic window that highlights a pretty image. Super fine glitter will usually cling to the plastic, but coarse glitter will shake loosely inside the window. I used a little of both for this card.

4 Cut the frame interiors. Measure and mark an interior area for each frame large enough to fit over your plastic window. Use the craft knife and metal ruler on a cutting mat to carefully slice out each interior. Make the edges of the top frame half the width of the bottom frame edges. My bottom frame has ½" (1.5cm)-wide edges and the top frame has ¼" (0.5cm)-wide edges.

5 Adhere the frames. Apply tape to the front of the bottom frame and to the back of the top frame on all four sides. Be sure the tape is right up against the inside edge of each frame so it seals around the edges of the window. Remove the paper backing from the tape, sandwich the plastic window evenly between the frames, and adhere it in place.

6 Place the seed beads. Place some seed beads on top of the scrapbook paper over the area(s) that will be covered with the window. In this example, my plastic piece actually had twelve little circle windows, so having a geometric pattern on the scrapbook paper made it easier to put the beads in the right spots.

7 Adhere the window. For this particular plastic window, I added a glue dot to each of the flat areas between the circles to keep the plastic flat against the card and prevent any beads from escaping the circles. Place glue dots on the necessary areas of the back of your window. Add tape to the back of the window frame, remove the paper backing, and adhere it to the card so it traps the beads.

8 Add embellishments. Use glue dots to add flat-back gems to the top of the card to cover up the glue dots on the back of the window that will be visible through the plastic. Adhere a sentiment charm if desired.

Greeting Card Set

STASH ITEMS: Scrapbook papers, buttons

I love my scrapbook papers—don't you? Nothing is more fun than picking them out, sheet by sheet, pad by pad. Many paper lines are released in coordinating groups of patterns and colors that look great together. These are perfect for creating sets of greeting cards or party invitations. Once you decide on a basic layout, it's quick and easy to whip up a batch of beautiful cards whenever you need a quick gift. See pages 40–43 for sample card templates.

SUPPLIES

* Ivory cardstock
* Solid color cardstock that coordinates with your scrapbook paper
* Scrapbook papers in two coordinating patterns
* Tape runner
* Ribbon
* Buttons
* Glue dots
* Metal ruler
* Bone folder
* Paper trimmer

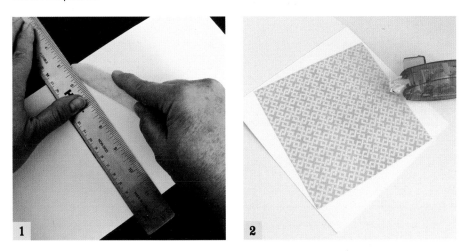

1   **Fold the card.** Trim a sheet of ivory cardstock to 6" x 12" (15 x 30.5cm). Score and fold it to a 6" (15cm) square card.

2   **Adhere the diagonal background.** Following the Off-Kilter template (see page 42), cut scrapbook paper with a small pattern to 5" (12.5cm) square for the diagonal background. Adhere it to the front of the card as shown, using tape runner in the corners.

Greeting Card Set *(continued)*

Look for nice blank envelopes at an office supply or stationery store, and then make cards to fit them.

When you're buying patterned papers, remember to also get solid color cardstock in a complementary color.

Use a chisel-tip marker to ink the edges of the card to give it a more polished look.

Use four different groups of papers and one template to make a set of four cards, each for a different occasion, recipient, or season. Wrap an extra-wide ribbon around the set for a gift.

Include some fancy postage stamps with the gift—make sure to add the extra postage required for cards that are heavy, bulky, or a nonstandard size.

3 **Create the focal image.** Cut a 4" (10cm) square from scrapbook paper with a large pattern. Trim around a focal image if possible. Then cut a 4¼" (3cm) square from coordinating solid color cardstock. Center the scrapbook paper on top of the cardstock and tape it down.

4 **Cut the ribbon strip.** Trim a strip of the solid color cardstock ¼" (0.5cm) wider total than your ribbon and 5" (12.5cm) long. Cut the ribbon to 5" (12.5cm) long.

5 **Adhere the ribbon strip.** Center the cardstock strip across the lower portion of the framed focal image. Fold each end of the strip over to the back of the focal image and secure them with tape. Repeat with the ribbon, centering it on top of the cardstock strip.

6 **Adhere the focal image.** Adhere the framed focal image in the center of the card, on top of the diagonal background.

7 **Add embellishments.** Use glue dots to stack two buttons together and adhere them to the ribbon.

Greeting Card Set *(continued)*

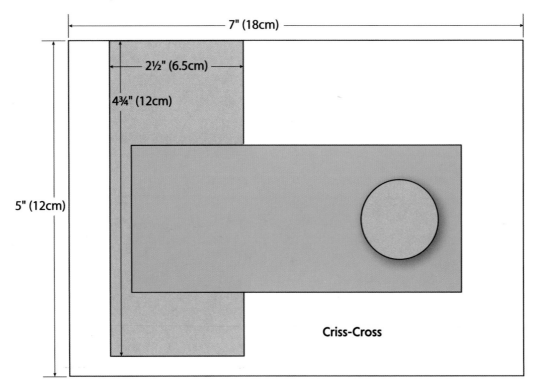

7" (18cm)

2½" (6.5cm)

4¾" (12cm)

5" (12cm)

Criss-Cross

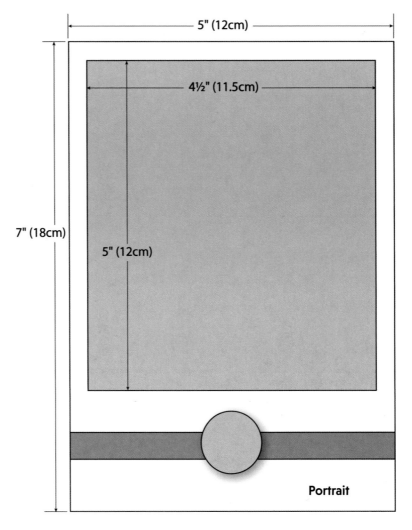

5" (12cm)

4½" (11.5cm)

7" (18cm)

5" (12cm)

Portrait

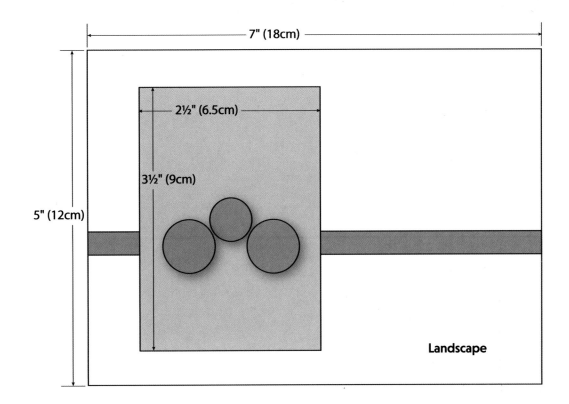

Landscape

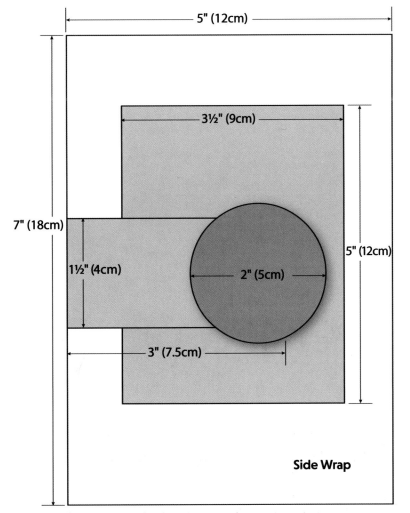

Side Wrap

Greeting Card Set *(continued)*

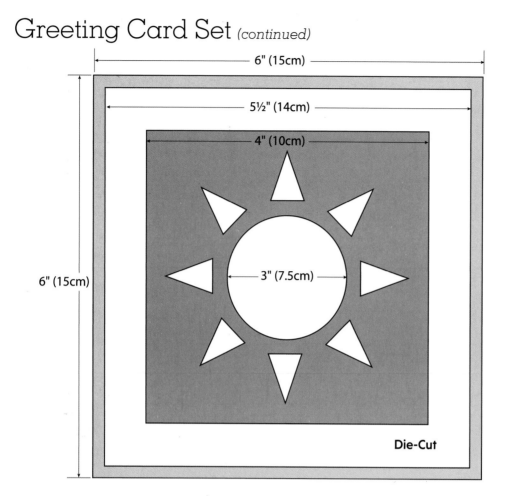

6" (15cm)

5½" (14cm)

4" (10cm)

3" (7.5cm)

6" (15cm)

Die-Cut

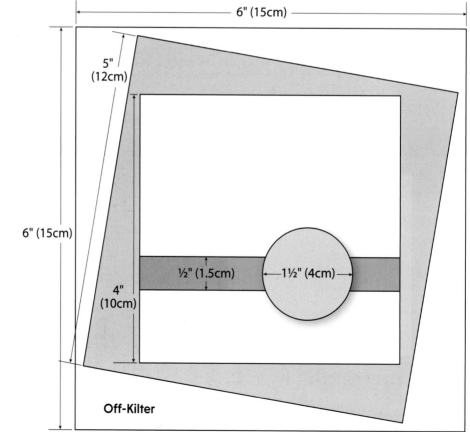

6" (15cm)

5" (12cm)

6" (15cm)

4" (10cm)

½" (1.5cm)

1½" (4cm)

Off-Kilter

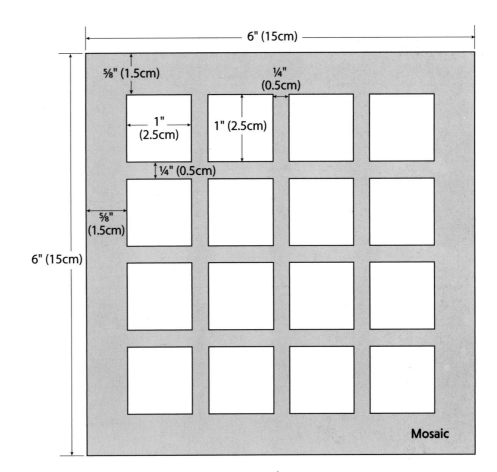

6" (15cm)

⅝" (1.5cm)

¼" (0.5cm)

1" (2.5cm)

1" (2.5cm)

¼" (0.5cm)

⅝" (1.5cm)

6" (15cm)

Mosaic

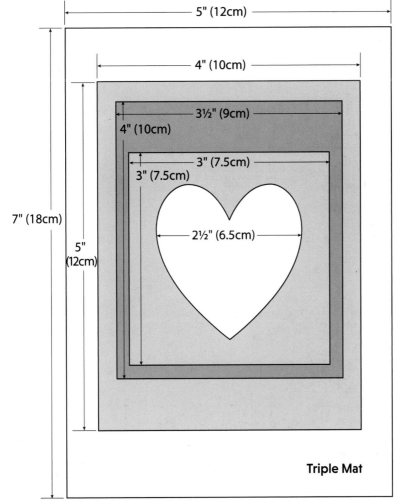

5" (12cm)

4" (10cm)

3½" (9cm)

4" (10cm)

3" (7.5cm)

3" (7.5cm)

2½" (6.5cm)

7" (18cm)

5" (12cm)

Triple Mat

CRAFT YOUR **STASH** 43

Waste Paint ATCs

✿ **STASH ITEMS: Paint, cardstock**

ATC stands for "artist trading card," and I have a personal collection of more than 300 from artists all over the world! ATCs are miniature works of art that people swap for fun, like baseball cards (yes, I have made more than 300 cards, too). They can be made with any medium, foundation, and technique; the only rule is that they must be 2½" x 3½" (6.5 x 9cm) in size. ATCs can also be used like tags or business cards to include with gifts or mailings. I like to have lots of cardstock with pre-painted backgrounds on hand to work with, so I use up any leftover paint I have from other craft projects to make them. I am pretty miserly with my paint—I just hate to waste it!

SUPPLIES
* Heavy white cardstock trimmed to 2½" x 3½" (6.5 x 9cm)
* Craft mat or parchment paper (work surface)
* Cosmetic wedge sponges
* Palette knife
* Rubber stamps
* Notched scraper tool (found in the paint/wallpaper section at hardware stores)
* Pencils with new eraser tops
* Stencils

1

2

1 **Stencil it.** Use a cosmetic sponge to dab a pattern on a card with a stencil.

2 **Stamp it.** Sponge some paint onto a rubber stamp and stamp it on a card.

Waste Paint ATCs *(continued)*

3

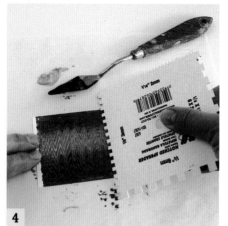
4

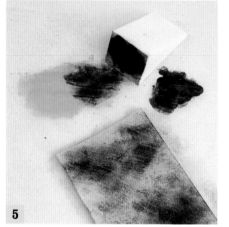
5

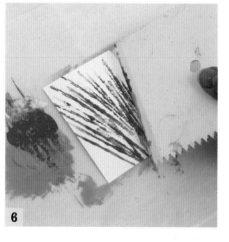
6

❧ TIPS ☙

Mix a few drops of fluid acrylic medium with the leftover paint to make it glide more easily when using the notched scraper tool.

Layer multiple colors of leftover paint on a card from light to dark. Sponge the lightest color on first, and then stencil a pattern on top with a medium color. Finish by adding dots or streaks in the darkest color as accents.

Use a hair dryer to speed-dry the paint on your cards if necessary.

When you're ready to make an ATC, pull out a pre-painted background card and add whatever you want on top of it—a découpage image, brads and gems, metal charms, wording, glitter, crackle medium, embossed stamping, stickers, etc.

Crop the edges of a painted card down by ¼" (0.5cm), and then adhere it in the center of a contrasting color of cardstock that is trimmed to ATC size to create a nice frame.

3 Dot it. Create polka dots with a pencil eraser.

4 Scrape it. Transfer a small puddle of paint(s) to the edge of a card with a palette knife. Then scrape the paint across the card with the notched tool to distribute it. Once the paint is distributed but still wet, pull the tool across the card again, moving it up and down as you go to make a zigzag pattern.

5 Sponge it. Dab two colors simultaneously onto a card with the cosmetic sponge.

6 Streak it. Drag or tap the straight edge of the scraper tool into the paint(s), and then tap the edge on a card to make streaks. You can also use the edge of an old credit card to do this.

Photo Cube Ornament

STASH ITEMS: Metal charms

I love nonseasonal ornaments! They're so pretty all year round hanging from a lamp switch, under a cabinet on a cup hook, at the bottom of an indoor plant hanger, or on curtain tiebacks as accents. Photo cube ornaments are especially nice because they're like mini scrapbooks. Each side can feature a different person, place, or event. Create a set to commemorate each day of your vacation or to highlight all the pictures you've been taking of beautiful flowers at the park.

SUPPLIES
* 3" (7.5cm) smooth foam cube
* Solid and patterned cardstock
* Themed stickers
* Metal charms and photo corners/frames
* Short ball-head straight pins
* Craft paint
* Paintbrush
* Tape runner
* Craft glue
* Heavy-duty contact glue
* Wood skewer
* Thin-gauge wire
* Beads and a charm
* Wire cutters
* Paper trimmer
* Personal photos

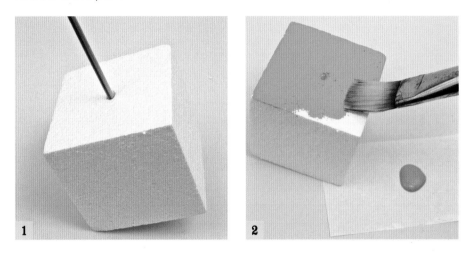

1 **Make a hole.** Make a hole through the center of the cube by slowly pushing a wood skewer straight down into the center of the cube from the top, pushing it all the way through the cube and out the bottom.

2 **Paint the cube.** Paint all sides of the cube with a color that coordinates with your cardstock. You can leave the skewer in the cube and use it like a handle to hold the cube while you paint it. Let it dry.

Photo Cube Ornament *(continued)*

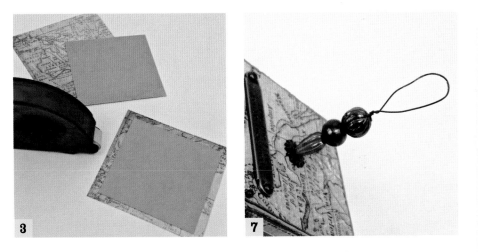

3

7

3 Cut the cardstock. Cut out four 2⅞" (7.5cm) squares from the patterned cardstock and four 2⅜" (6cm) squares from the solid color cardstock. Center and adhere a solid color square on top of each patterned square using tape runner. These will serve as double mats for your photos.

4 Prepare the photos. Crop and cut four photos to 2" (5cm) squares. Adhere one to the center of each double mat with tape runner. Lay out the matted photos with your metal frames and charms and decide how you want to embellish each photo. Then use contact glue to adhere the charms and frames into place as desired. Let everything dry.

5 Attach the photos. Adhere a photo arrangement to each side of the cube with craft glue and let them dry. Push pins into the four corners of each double mat to accent them. Push the pins into the cube at a slight inward angle so they don't accidentally poke out of the edge of the cube.

6 Cover the top and bottom. Cut two more 2⅞" (7.5cm) squares from the patterned cardstock to glue on the top and bottom of the cube, along with more metal charms. Poke a hole through the center of each paper to access the hole you made through the cube.

7 Add a hanger. Thread a 12" (30.5cm) length of wire through the cube. Add a few beads to the ends of the wire extending above and below the cube. Finish the wire end above the cube by twisting it into a loop for hanging. Finish the wire end below the cube by adding a charm dangle below the beads and twisting the wire to finish it off.

❧ TIPS ☙

Use a paintbrush to spread your glue evenly onto each photo and piece of cardstock, making sure it goes all the way out to the edges for better adhesion. Be sure to rinse the brush in water immediately afterward.

Instead of hanging your photo cubes as ornaments, skip step 7 and stack them like blocks on a shelf or on the coffee table.

You can also work with wood, plastic, or papier mâché cubes instead of foam.

Personalize a cube for a wedding or baby shower gift. Include a description of what will be a "belated" gift in your card, and then shoot some photos at the event to work with. Deliver the cube shortly after the shower—so thoughtful!

Suncatcher

✿ **STASH ITEMS: Beads, recycled packaging**

A sparkly suncatcher hanging in the kitchen window somehow makes doing the dishes a little more pleasant, doesn't it? It's especially nice when the distraction of shimmering glints comes from something you made yourself with easy knots and your favorite beads. And who doesn't love turning trash into treasure! This project recycles a soup can lid and empty plastic packaging.

SUPPLIES
* 30 or more small, faceted beads (crystal or plastic)
* 9 medium-size focal beads (8 of the same size and weight)
* Large crystal teardrop bead
* 0.08 or 1.0mm clear elastic beading cord
* Ten 1"–2" (2.5–5cm)-long eye pins
* Sturdy, clear plastic packaging
* Alcohol inks in 4 bright colors
* Alcohol ink applicator and felt pads
* ⅛" (0.5cm) heavy-duty hole punch
* 9 large jump rings
* 1 small jump ring
* 1"–2" (2.5–5cm) length of small chain
* Soup can lid (use a side-access can opener to eliminate sharp edges)
* Scissors
* Fine-point marker
* Flat-nose pliers
* Round-nose pliers
* Wire cutters

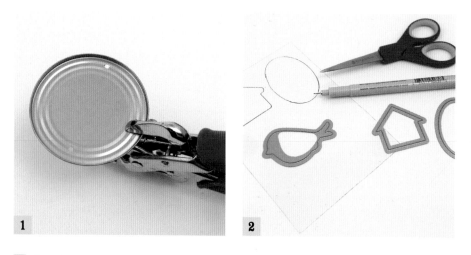

1

1 Punch the holes. Punch nine holes in the soup can lid. Punch four along the outer edge at 12:00, 3:00, 6:00, and 9:00. Punch four holes closer to the center, positioning them between the outside holes you punched previously. Punch one hole in the center. Use a large nail and hammer on a block of wood to make the center hole if the throat of your hole punch is too shallow. See the hole punch diagram below.

2 Cut the shapes. Trace and cut out eight shapes from a sheet of plastic packaging. Make four shapes roughly the same size for the outside holes of the suncatcher. The four shapes for the inside holes can vary in size.

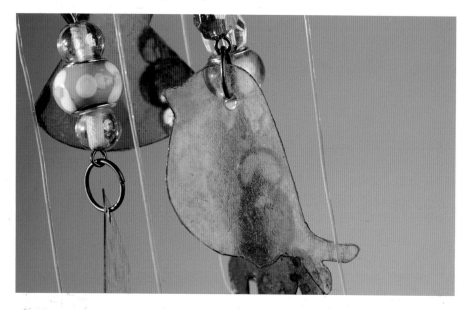

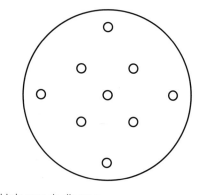

Hole punch diagram

Suncatcher *(continued)*

3 **Color the shapes.** Punch a hole at the top of each shape. Then color both sides with alcohol ink. I colored mine in pairs, making two pink, two blue, two citrus, and two caramel. Use a tapping motion with the ink applicator to achieve a slightly marbled look.

4 **Make the beaded eye pins.** String a focal bead between two small faceted beads onto an eye pin. Trim the end of the eye pin to approximately ⅜″ (1cm) and use the round-nose pliers to twist it into a loop. Repeat to create seven more beaded eye pins. Attach a plastic shape to each beaded eye pin with a large jump ring.

5 **Tie on the beading cord.** Using double overhand knots, tie 18″ (45.5cm) lengths of beading cord to the top loops of the eye pins attached to the four shapes for the outside holes of the suncatcher. Pull the knots tight and trim away the short ends. Repeat to tie 12″ (30.5cm) lengths of beading cord to the loops of the eye pins attached to the shapes for the inside holes.

6 **Add beads.** Thread a set of three beads onto each of the 18″ (45.5cm) cords. Position the beads about 6″ (15cm) above the eye pins. Tie an overhand knot in the cord above and below each set of beads to hold them in place. If desired, repeat with the 12″ (30.5cm) cords.

7 **Attach the outside cords.** Tie an overhand knot about 3″ (7.5cm) above the set of three beads on one of the 18″ (45.5cm) cords and thread on a bead. Then thread the end of the cord up through an outside hole in the lid. Thread on a bead and tie a knot above it. The line will be suspended from the lid with a bead above and below the lid. Adjust the knots and beads so the shape at the end of the line is hanging down about 10″ (25.5cm) from the lid. Repeat with the remaining 18″ (45.5cm) cords and outside holes. Don't worry if they aren't all exactly the same length; a little stagger is nice!

8 **Tie the ends.** To create the tension in the outside cords that's needed for the suncatcher to hang straight, tie the ends of the 18″ (45.5cm) cords together in opposing pairs tautly over the center point in the lid. Trim the ends and attach a small jump ring over the cords where they intersect.

OVERHAND KNOT: For a double overhand knot, tie an overhand knot, and then tie a second one on top of the first.

9

10

9 Attach the inside cords. Thread the end of a 12" (30.5cm) cord up through an inside hole in the lid. Thread on a bead and tie a knot above it so the shape at the end of the cord is hanging down 4"–6" (10–15cm) from the lid. The bead will be on top of the lid. Repeat with the remaining 12" (30.5cm) cords and inside holes, staggering the cord lengths so each shape can be seen. The top of the lid will look like the image above left when you are finished with this step.

10 Attach the center dangle. For the center dangle, follow step 4 to create a beaded eye pin. Attach the beaded eye pin to the teardrop bead with a large jump ring. Attach the other end of the eye pin to the short length of chain. Attach the other end of the chain to the loop of another eye pin. Thread the end of this eye pin up through the center hole in the can lid and through the small jump ring you attached in step 8. Twist the end of the eye pin into a double loop. If desired, attach a hook to the double loop for hanging the suncatcher.

·⋞ TIPS ⋟·

If you have crimping pliers and crimp beads or tubes, use them instead of knots to secure each eye pin to the beading cord for a cleaner look. If desired, you can also place crimp tubes before and after each set of beads to hold them in place. But believe me, nobody will grade you on your knots or their little tails...all they'll see is color and sparkle!

Have fun using a random selection of beads. Your cords don't have to match—variety is cool!

Try blending two colors of alcohol ink to make different shades or create a two-tone mottled effect. Use an alcohol ink blending solution to remove color or bleed colors together.

Try creating a monochromatic look with one color of ink and all matching beads.

Disguise the soup can lid by gluing circles of pretty cardstock to each side before punching the holes.

Wind Chimes

❀ **STASH ITEMS: Shells, sea glass**

It's hard to pass up those pretty shells or chunks of sea glass you find on the beach. You can also buy them at the craft store for a particular project, but they usually come in bags by the dozens or even hundreds—you can't purchase one small shell at a time. If you have an overabundance of shells and sea glass, this project is a fun way to bring a bit of the beach to your own backyard. Their clickety-clack sound is simply sweet in a nice breeze.

SUPPLIES
* ❋ Medium-size shells
* ❋ Small chunks of sea glass
* ❋ 0.8 or 1.0mm clear elastic beading cord
* ❋ Sturdy branch or thick, paper-covered armature wire
* ❋ Flat silver pendant bails
* ❋ Small silver beads with holes large enough to fit two strands of beading cord
* ❋ Heavy-duty contact glue
* ❋ Round-nose pliers
* ❋ Scissors

1 **Prepare the shells.** Select enough shells and sea glass to fill up your branch as desired. Wipe them clean with a damp paper towel and let them dry.

2 **Attach the bails.** Bend a pendant bail in half around the pliers, and then glue each side to the edge of a shell or piece of sea glass. Pinch and hold the bail in place with the pliers for a minute or two until the glue sets. Repeat to attach bails to the remaining shells and glass pieces. Let the glue dry completely according to the manufacturer's instructions.

2

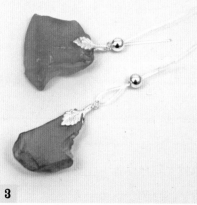

3

4

3 **Attach the beading cord.** Cut a 14" (35.5cm) length of beading cord for each shell and glass piece. Slide a silver bead onto the end of a cord, then thread the end through a bail, and tie a double overhand knot below the bead. Slide the tail up through the bead and trim it. Secure the knot with a tiny drop of glue if desired. Repeat for all the shells and glass pieces.

4 **Tie on the chimes.** Tie the shell and glass chimes onto the branch or wire using double overhand knots, alternating shells with sea glass. Make sure all the pieces touch each other.

5 **Finish.** Take another length of beading cord and tie each end to each end of the branch. Hang the wind chime in your favorite spot outside. Bring it inside during severe weather.

⊰ TIPS ⊱

Try using metal tags or small flat washers instead of sea glass.

Add small beads to each cord for more sparkle and pops of color.

Wind chimes are super cute hanging indoors too—just tickle them every once in a while!

Door Plaque

✿ **STASH ITEMS: Rub-on transfers**

Doors need just as much adorning as any other surface in your home—why should walls and refrigerators get all the fun? Create a door plaque with a layered collage of your favorite rub-on quotes, scrolls, and images. Design a personalized theme for each of your family member's bedrooms, or put your favorite inspirational quotes where you can enjoy reading them every day. Make your plaques double sided so you can flip them around whenever the mood strikes you!

SUPPLIES
* ❋ Unfinished wood die-cut shape
* ❋ Rub-on transfers
* ❋ Wooden craft stick
* ❋ Sanding block
* ❋ Paint marker
* ❋ Clear gloss glazing medium (fluid)
* ❋ Paintbrush
* ❋ Flat-back gems
* ❋ Thin-gauge wire
* ❋ Beads
* ❋ Scissors

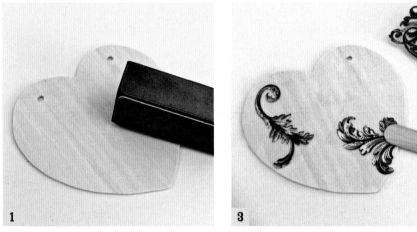

1 **Sand the edges.** Smooth off any rough edges on your wood plaque with a sanding block. Wipe away all the sawdust from the surface when you're finished.

2 **Arrange your rub-ons.** Cut out your selected rub-ons and arrange them to fill the plaque's surface however you like. Most rub-ons are fairly opaque, so look for interesting ways to layer words on top of images, solid flowers on top of scrolls, thin line art on top of large solid areas, etc.

3 **Apply the rub-ons.** Carefully apply the rub-ons to the plaque one at a time with the craft stick, starting with the bottom layer.

Door Plaque *(continued)*

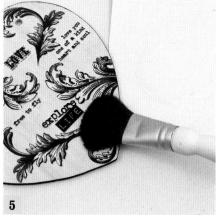

4 **Finish the edges.** Color the edges of the plaque with a paint marker.

5 **Apply glazing medium.** Brush the glazing medium very gently and slowly over the whole surface of the plaque to seal it.

6 **Embellish.** While the medium is still wet, place a few flat-back gems on the plaque (the medium will act as a glue) to accent your design.

7 **Add a hanger.** If the plaque has pre-drilled holes for hanging like my heart plaque does, find beads that are larger than the holes. Thread a bead onto a 12″ (30.5cm) length of thin-gauge wire, placing it in the center of the wire, and then fold the wire in half around the bead. Thread both ends of the wire through the left hole in the plaque from front to back, using the bead as a stopper. Repeat for the right hole. Bend both wires up and twist the ends into a loop for hanging.

·❧ TIPS ❧·

If there are no pre-drilled holes in the plaque for hanging, drill them yourself before sanding.

Other options for hanging your plaque include attaching a self-adhesive picture hanger to the back, taping or stapling a loop of embroidery floss or wire to the back, or gluing the plaque onto a wide ribbon that can be pinned to the door.

Add some shimmer by lightly sprinkling some clear, fine glitter over the glazing medium while it's still wet.

Some rub-ons have a shelf life—I have found older rub-ons that have been sitting in my stash for a really long time will not transfer cleanly. If possible, test one of the rub-ons from the pack on a piece of paper before trying to transfer the one you want to the plaque.

Cut a large scroll or detailed floral image into smaller parts to accent or fill in specific areas of your collage.

Vacation Shadow Box

STASH ITEMS: Travel ephemera, stickers

Ticket stubs, travel brochures, matchbooks, postcards, menus, subway tokens, swizzle sticks, coins from far-off lands...we keep every little thing from our vacations when the trip is really special. Combine some of these precious collected items with themed papers and embellishments to create a unique diorama that commemorates each of your trips. Display several together on a bookshelf, or place a single one on your desk to remind yourself that vacation time is coming!

SUPPLIES

* Square papier mâché box with lid
* Patterned and/or themed scrapbook papers
* Cardstock
* Maps, ephemera, and stickers
* Personal photos
* Craft paint
* Découpage medium
* Craft knife
* Metal ruler
* Cutting mat
* Paintbrush
* Scissors
* Paper trimmer
* Clear acetate
* Flat and dimensional glue dots
* Flat-back gems and charms

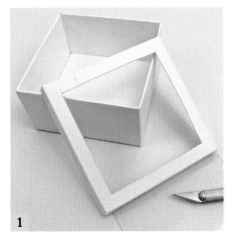

1

5

1 Cut the lid. Slice a square out of the center of the lid with the craft knife and ruler, leaving about a ½" (1.5cm) border.

2 Paint the lid. Paint the lid inside and out and let it dry. Then brush on a coat of découpage medium to seal it.

3 Create the window. Cut a sheet of clear acetate to secure to the underside of the lid as a window. Cut it about ¼" (0.5cm) larger on all sides than the opening in the lid, and use several small glue dots on each side to adhere it in place.

4 Cover the sides of the box. Cut the maps or scrapbook papers that match your vacation theme into pieces that fit the inner and outer sides of the box. Use découpage medium to attach them to the sides of the box.

5 Cover the bottom of the box. Cut a piece of scrapbook paper to fit the inside bottom of your box. Adhere a collage of stickers and/or ephemera to it and glue it in place.

Vacation Shadow Box (continued)

6

6 Make a cutout. Set the box on its side so the collage is upright and facing out. This forms the background for your diorama. Select a photo, such as a person or a monument, and adhere it to cardstock. Trim closely around the edges of the photo, leaving a 1" (2.5cm) tab of cardstock at the bottom. Fold the tab back at a 90º angle and glue it to the inside of your box in front of the collage so the cutout is in the foreground.

7 Embellish. Add a few charms or other embellishments with dimensional glue dots to accent the inside and outside of the box.

❧ TIPS ❧

Thread some chain or beading cord through a small hole in the top of the box and use it to hang a charm inside the box in front of the collage.

Use a self-adhesive plate hanger tab to mount the box on a wall. If you're worried the lid might fall off, stick a couple adhesive hook-and-loop tape dots in the corners to secure it.

Place a battery-operated tea light inside the box to illuminate your scene.

Treasure Box

✿ **STASH ITEMS: Vintage brooch, broken jewelry**

There are millions of inexpensive brooches at every thrift shop, secondhand store, and flea market, and if you love vintage or retro bling, they're hard to pass up. But how many brooches can you really wear? They'll probably end up at the bottom of your jewelry box with your broken earrings or necklaces. This treasure box is a beautiful way to keep that bling alive!

SUPPLIES
- ❋ Unfinished wood or papier mâché box with lid (hinged or separate)
- ❋ Brooches and/or broken jewelry
- ❋ Assorted small beads, metal charms, and flat-back gems
- ❋ Metallic craft paint
- ❋ White gesso
- ❋ Heavy-duty contact glue
- ❋ Felt
- ❋ Extra tacky double-sided tape
- ❋ Paintbrush
- ❋ Wire cutters
- ❋ Scissors

1 Paint the lid. Paint the entire box and lid, inside and out, with a coat of white gesso. Let it dry, and then add two coats of metallic paint. Let everything dry between coats.

2 Prepare the jewelry pieces. Remove, bend back, or cut off the pins or prongs on the back of each jewelry piece so the backs are flat.

3 Glue the jewelry. Arrange and glue the large jewelry pieces and charms on top of the lid. Fill in the open areas between them with small beads and gems. Let everything dry completely. If you're working with a papier mâché box, place a large wood stamp block under the lid so it doesn't cave in when you press glued items into place.

4 Line the box. Trim the felt into pieces to fit the inner sides and bottom of your box and the underside of the lid. Adhere the felt to the inside of the box and lid with the double-sided tape. You can also use craft glue for more permanence. Apply a very thin coat to the interior sides of the box so it doesn't soak through the felt.

❧ **TIPS** ❧

If you want to use a brooch or pendant that has a convex curve to it, try pressing and gluing some air-dry polymer clay into the curve of the back to create a flat surface to glue to your box lid.

Try arranging and gluing a few gems or small jewelry pieces to the sides of the box, or glue an extra-special piece to the inside of the lid.

No need to wrap this if it's a gift! Tuck a handmade necklace, some candy, or a gift card inside for the recipient.

With a papier mâché box, you can cut a slot in the lid to fit the pin on the back of a brooch. The brooch can be nested in the slot when you're not using it and removed from the lid when you want to wear it.

Lariat Bead Necklace

✿ STASH ITEMS: Beads

You can wear this lariat necklace with just about any outfit—it's so versatile! There are no rules—all sizes, colors, and types of beads are welcome. Use up all those stray single beads and leftovers from other projects.

SUPPLIES
* ✱ Beads, beads, and more beads
* ✱ 30" (76cm) of 0.7mm clear elastic beading cord
* ✱ Large decorative ring
* ✱ Head pin
* ✱ Round-nose pliers
* ✱ Scissors
* ✱ Large piece of felt

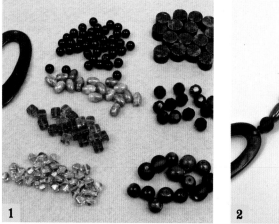

1 **Prepare the beads.** Lay your beads out on the felt and remove any that are too big to fit through the ring. Have fun mixing up the colors to achieve an overall random look.

2 **Start stringing the beads.** Tie one end of the beading cord to the ring with a double overhand knot. Begin stringing beads onto the beading cord. Thread the tail from the overhand knot through the first few beads you string to hide it. For every bead you string above the ring, set aside a bead just like it so both side of the necklace will match.

3 **Finish stringing the beads.** Continue stringing beads onto the cord. When you reach the center of the cord, start stringing the matching beads you set aside previously in reverse order.

4 **Attach the dangle.** When all the beads are strung, set the necklace aside. String a large finishing bead on the head pin and bend the top into a loop with the round-nose pliers. Tie the end of the cord to the loop in the head pin with a double overhand knot. Thread the tail through the beads above the knot to hide it.

❖ TIPS ❖

Adjust the length of the beading cord as desired to make a longer or shorter lariat.

The ring you use can be made of plastic, metal, shell, or wood. If you don't find something you like in your stash or at your favorite bead retailer, look for interesting rings where macramé supplies or sewing notions are sold. A child's bangle bracelet might work, or check the hardware store for plain metal rings.

If you're working with small beads, a plain wedding band would make a beautiful ring.

Mosaic Tile Backdrop

❀ **STASH ITEMS: Chipboard**

Give one of your special *tchotchkes* center stage with a book cover-style backdrop filled with a mosaic grid of chipboard tiles. Perhaps it's a porcelain figurine, a small statue, or a carved wooden bird—whatever sentimental souvenir you love the most deserves an extra-special home on your shelf.

SUPPLIES
* ❋ Extra-thick chipboard, illustration board, or book board
* ❋ Regular chipboard (recycled from paper pads, packaging, etc.)
* ❋ Dimensional adhesive foam squares
* ❋ Craft paint in a dark color
* ❋ Solid or patterned duct tape that matches your paint
* ❋ High-gloss glazing medium
* ❋ Découpage medium
* ❋ Patterned scrapbook papers or personal photos
* ❋ Paper trimmer
* ❋ Scissors
* ❋ Craft knife
* ❋ Metal ruler
* ❋ Cutting mat
* ❋ Paintbrush
* ❋ Chisel-tip paint marker
* ❋ Parchment paper

1 **Determine the size.** Use the size of your display item to determine the size of your folded two-panel backdrop. Each panel should be 1"–2" (2.5–5cm) taller than the display item and at least twice the width. Even-numbered dimensions will be easiest to work with, so round up as needed.

2 **Prepare the panels.** Using a craft knife and ruler (or paper trimmer), cut two panels of board stock to the dimensions you calculated in step 1. Paint both sides and the edges of each panel a dark color that will contrast nicely with your color scheme for the tiles. The paint will show in between the tiles like grout.

3 **Select the collage paper.** Decide what papers and/or photos you want to cut into tiles and collage onto the panel backdrop. Select enough papers to cover the surface area of your backdrop panels. Adhere the papers onto sheets of chipboard with découpage medium. Let them dry on parchment paper. Apply a thin coat of glaze to seal the paper and make it glossy. Allow the glaze to air dry.

Mosaic Tile Backdrop *(continued)*

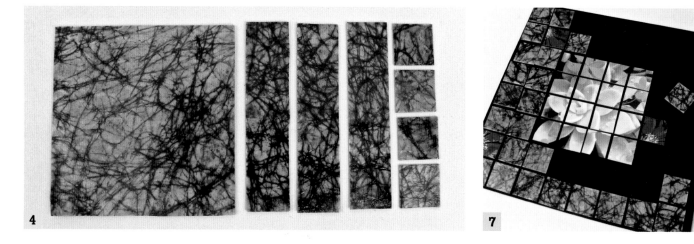

4

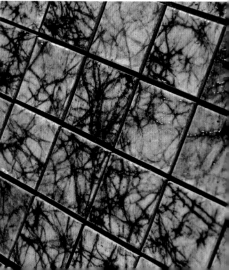

7

4   Cut the tiles. Determine the number and size of tiles you'd like to cut to cover the background panels. For example, if your panels are 8" x 8" (20.5 x 20.5cm), you might cut 64 tiles ⅞" (2cm) square or 16 tiles 1⅞" (5cm) square for each panel. Cut each piece of chipboard into tiles of your desired size. Make this easy by first cutting strips the width of your tile size, and then cutting the strips into squares. Lay out each tile on your work surface as you go.

5   Map out the design. Once all the tiles are cut, map out the design of your mosaic, and arrange the tiles as you would like to glue them onto the panels.

6   Prepare the tiles. Ink the edges of each tile with a paint marker in a color that matches the paint you used for the panels. Allow everything to dry. Then apply an adhesive foam square to the back of each tile in the center. Make sure you keep your tiles in order on your work surface as you do this to keep your design intact.

7   Attach the tiles. Adhere each tile into position on the panels. Space the tiles as desired based on the size. Following the example from step 4, if you have 8" x 8" (20.5 x 20.5cm) panels and cut ⅞" (2cm) tiles, you can space them out evenly by leaving about ⅛" (0.5cm) between them.

8   Connect the panels. After both panels are tiled, place them face down on your work surface with the edges touching. Cut a piece of duct tape to the same height of the panels and attach it to the panels over the place where the edges touch, like a spine on a book. This will connect the panels and allow you to set them up behind your display item like an open book.

⋇ TIPS ⋇

If using photos printed by an inkjet printer for the tiles, test the glazing medium on one to be sure it won't react with your printer ink and smear the image.

Tiles can be cut into diamonds or rectangles instead of squares.

Use craft glue instead of foam adhesive squares if you don't like the dimensional look.

Altered CD Art

STASH ITEMS: Recycled CDs, scrapbook supplies

Instead of hanging a plant or a mobile from the ceiling, hang a strand of artfully altered CDs! I had a stash of old CDs from junk mail, old software, music I didn't like anymore, and temporary file storage sitting around for ages. I just knew I'd figure out something fun to make with those plastic circles that are so lustrous on one side. Hang the strand in front of a window or sliding glass door to enjoy the reflective qualities of the shiny sides of the CDs.

SUPPLIES
* ☀ 5 old CDs
* ☀ Scrapbook papers and cardstock
* ☀ Stickers and sentiments
* ☀ Paper flowers and leaves
* ☀ Tags and die-cuts
* ☀ Flat-back gems and charms
* ☀ Craft glue
* ☀ Paintbrush
* ☀ Flat and dimensional glue dots
* ☀ Large jump rings
* ☀ Beading pliers
* ☀ 8"–14" (20.5–35.5cm) length of small-link chain
* ☀ Small "S" hook
* ☀ Pencil
* ☀ Scissors
* ☀ Heavy-duty hole punch

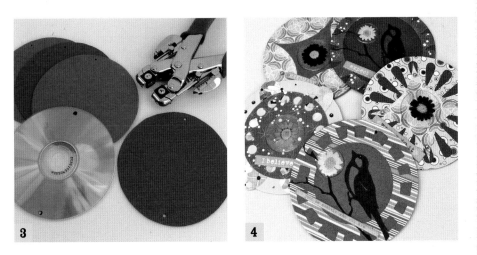

1 Plan your design. Each CD can be uniquely decorated, but you'll want the whole strand to have a cohesive look. Start by selecting an overall color palette and theme that complements your home décor, such as florals, steampunk, modern metallics, shabby chic, vintage, animal prints, etc.

2 Attach the background paper. Trace and cut out a circle of background paper for each CD. Glue each circle to the printed side of a CD. Make sure you brush the glue all the way out to the edges of the paper for a clean seal. Let everything dry.

3 Punch the holes. Create a punch template by tracing a CD onto paper. Cut out the circle and punch a hole at 12:00 and another at 6:00, keeping both holes fairly close to the edge. Use the template and a pencil to mark where to punch the holes in each of your paper-covered CDs, and then punch them. Using the template will ensure your CDs hang straight.

4 Decorate the CDs. Finish each CD any way you'd like—try layering papers for dimension and add an inspiring sentiment to each one. You might find it easiest to work with a scrapbook paper collection that has a pad of coordinating papers with matching embellishments.

5 Connect the CDs. Attach the chain to the top hole of the first CD. Then, use the jump rings to connect the first CD to the remaining CDs to create a chain. Attach a charm or dangle to the bottom hole of the last CD. Use the "S" hook to hang your CD chain from a ceiling hook.

Altered CD Art (continued)

✥ TIPS ✥

A die-cutting machine comes in handy for this project. I used mine to cut circular designs for the background papers, as well as for some of the embellishments.

Treat the CDs like mini scrapbook layouts and feature a photo on each one.

Hanging CDs are a great way to show off your favorite silk and paper flowers. Take them out of the vase and let them spin in the air!

Yarn Art Wall Hanging

✽ **STASH ITEMS: Yarn, old wool sweater**

Got a wool sweater you can't wear anymore because the moths took a couple nibbles? Turn it into a super cute accent for your wall using needle felting. It's a super easy craft to learn, and all the stress of the day just melts away every time you punch those needles into the wool. Doodle your way around the surface with a few strands of fuzzy yarn, and have fun!

SUPPLIES
* Old wool sweater (not too holey!)
* Thick fuzzy yarn
* 5-needle punch
* Large piece of dense upholstery foam at least 2" (5cm) thick
* Scissors
* 9" or 10" (23 or 25.5cm) embroidery hoop

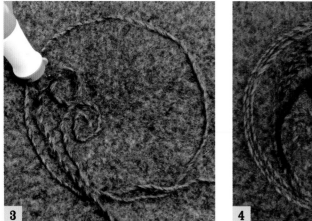

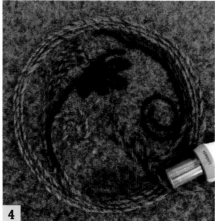

1 Cut the background fabric. Lay your sweater out flat and cut out a 10"–12" (25.5–30.5cm) square piece without holes.

2 Plan your design. Work out a doodle design to add to your square wool piece with the yarn. Use the pattern on page 75 or create one of your own. Try using long, continuous lines to reduce the number of loose ends that need to be punched down into the wool. Make sure your design fits within the size of your embroidery hoop, allowing 1" (2.5cm) or so of space around the edges of the design for a border.

3 Begin punching the design. Place the wool on top of the upholstery foam. Take a long strand of yarn and place one end at the starting point of your doodle design. Use the needle punch to punch the end of the yarn down into the wool at the starting point. Continue positioning the yarn on the wool according to your design and using the punch to secure it to the wool. Always punch straight up and down—the needles can break if you punch at too much of an angle.

4 Continue punching the design. Continue working your doodle in this way, punching the yarn a little bit at a time to lightly anchor your design to the wool. If necessary, you will still be able to pull up the yarn and reposition it. Pull the wool up off the foam every few punches to prevent locking too many yarn fibers into the foam.

Yarn Art Wall Hanging *(continued)*

6

5 **Secure the design.** Once you have completed the yarn doodle, pull the wool up off the foam, turn the foam over so it's firm and flat, and lay the wool back down on top of it. Go over the yarn design with the needle punch repeatedly to lock the fibers of the yarn into the wool. The more you punch, the flatter the yarn will become against the wool. Be sure to pull the wool up off the foam a few times as you work.

6 **Trim the wool.** Secure the wool in the embroidery hoop, centering the design inside it. Trim off the excess wool around the outer edges of the hoop. Display your creation on a shelf or add a loop of embroidery floss or ribbon at the top to hang it on the wall.

Start

Skinny Fabric Bulletin Board

✿ **STASH ITEMS: Ribbon, fat quarters**

Most bulletin boards, both store bought and handmade, seem to be squares or rectangles of various sizes. But often I have found that a long, skinny bulletin board would be so much handier. It can hang on the back of a door or on that narrow portion of your wall where nothing else fits. Turn it on its side and it fits nicely on the wall right above your desk, too!

SUPPLIES
* Solid core wood closet shelf, 8"–10" (20.5–25.5cm) wide, 3'–4' (91.5–123cm) long
* 3 coordinating fat quarters of fabric
* Quilt batting
* Several yards of narrow ribbon
* Staple gun
* ⅜" (1cm) staples
* Scissors
* Sewing machine
* Iron

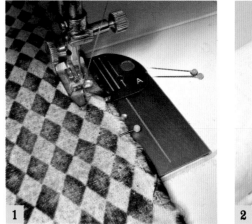

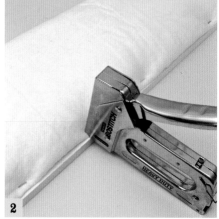

1 **Sew the fabric.** Sew the three 18" x 22" (45.5 x 56cm) fat quarters together along the 22" (56cm) sides using a ¼" (0.5cm) seam allowance to create a three-panel piece that is 53" (134.5cm) wide by 22" (56cm) tall overall. When you wrap this fabric around the shelf, you'll see more of the center panel than the two side panels, so place your favorite focal fabric in the center. Press the seams and iron out any wrinkles and folds.

2 **Attach the batting.** Cut or fold four layers of batting to the size of the shelf. Place the batting layers on top of the shelf, aligning the edges, and use the staple gun to staple them in place.

3

5

TIPS

Attach items to the bulletin board by tucking them behind the ribbon or using decorative straight pins pushed into the padded areas at an angle.

Nail or screw picture hangers into the back of the bulletin board on either a short side or a long side, depending on whether you want to hang it vertically or horizontally. It looks great just leaning against the wall, too.

3 **Attach the fabric.** Lay the fabric, right side down, on a sturdy table. Place the shelf on top of the fabric in the center with the padded side down. Starting with one of the long sides, wrap the edge of the fabric over the shelf to the back, pulling it taut. Fold the edge of the fabric under and staple it to the back of the shelf. Make sure you keep the seams in the fabric straight and parallel the to ends of the shelf as you do this. Repeat for the other long side.

4 **Finish the ends.** Trim off the excess fabric at the short ends of the shelf. Then fold and miter the fabric at the corners, wrap it around to the back of the shelf, and staple it in place at each short end.

5 **Attach the ribbon.** Wrap the ribbon around the shelf tautly to create a crisscross pattern. Staple the ribbon in place on the back of the shelf.

Easy-Sew Fabric Gift Bags

STASH ITEMS: Fat quarters

If you collect yummy fat quarters like candy, you should never, ever have to buy wrapping paper again. For those of you who might not know, a "fat quarter" is a pre-cut piece of fabric that measures 18" x 22" (45.5 x 56cm). Fat quarters are the perfect size for stitching up gift bags with just a few straight seams. The colorful fabric patterns make any present more exciting, plus these bags are reusable—it's great to be green, right? They're also great for packing delicates and jewelry when you travel.

SUPPLIES
* 4 fat quarters (makes 4 bags)
* Iron
* Sewing machine
* Straight pins
* Ribbons

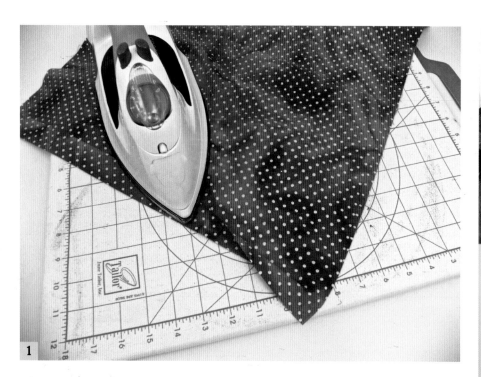

Large Bag
Finished size: 17½" x 20¾" (44.5 x 52.5cm)

1 Hem the top. Make a hem on one of the 18" (45.5cm) sides of a fat quarter by folding the edge over (wrong sides facing) by 1" (2.5cm) and pressing it in place with a hot iron. Repeat with a second fat quarter. Stitch each hem in place. This hemmed edge will be the top edge of your bag.

2 Pin the fabric. Lay the two hemmed fabrics on top of one another, right sides together, with the hemmed edges at the top. Pin the pieces together along the bottom and sides.

3 Stitch the bag. Sew the two pieces together along the sides and bottom using a ¼" (0.5cm) seam allowance. Remove the pins, turn the bag right side out, and press it flat.

⚜ TIP ⚜

Four fat quarters will make four bags: one large, one medium, and two small.

Easy-Sew Fabric Gift Bags *(continued)*

Medium Bag

Finished size: 10¾" x 16¾" (27.5 x 42.5cm)

1 Hem the top. Press and stitch a 1" (2.5cm) hem on one of the 22" (56cm) sides of a fat quarter. This will be the top edge of your bag. Fold the fabric in half to 11" x 17" (28 x 43cm) with wrong sides together and pin along the bottom and open edge.

2 Stitch the bag. Sew the fabric together along the bottom and open side using a ¼" (0.5cm) seam allowance. Remove the pins, turn the bag right side out, and press it flat.

Small Bags

Finished size: 8¾" x 9¾" (22 x 25cm)

1 Hem the top. Cut a fat quarter in half to two 11" x 18" (28 x 45.5cm) pieces. Press and stitch a 1" (2.5cm) hem on one of the 18" (45.5cm) sides of each piece. This will be the top edge of your bag. Fold each piece in half to 9" x 10" (23 x 25.5cm) with wrong sides together and pin along the bottom and open edge.

2 Stitch the bags. Sew each piece of fabric separately, stitching along the bottom and open side using a ¼" (0.5cm) seam allowance. Remove the pins, turn the bags right side out, and press them flat.

❊ TIPS ❊

Place a gift inside the bag, then gather the top of the bag and tie a ribbon around it. Iron the bag first with spray starch at the top so the gathered fabric stands up nicely above the ribbon.

For a flat gift, like a book, place it in the bag and fold the top of the bag to one side. Then tie a ribbon around the outside as if it were a box.

Open the side seams at the top edge of the bag at the hem. Thread a long ribbon or cord into the channel between the top of the bag and the hem stitch, and use it like a drawstring to close the bag.

Add stuffing, batting, or packing peanuts to the bag with your gift to make the bag look full and poufy when you close it.

Reversible Square Placemats

STASH ITEMS: Fat quarters

I really like the way square placemats look on the dining table. They peek out from under the place settings just enough to add festive color without taking over the whole tabletop. Square placemats allow the centerpiece (and the food!) to shine. And here's the real bonus...these placemats are reversible! Don't you just love a good two-fer?

SUPPLIES
- ✳ 4 fat quarters, 2 each of 2 patterns (makes 2 placemats)
- ✳ 1½–2 yd. (150–200cm) flannel, any color
- ✳ Rotary cutter
- ✳ Acrylic quilter's ruler
- ✳ Cutting mat
- ✳ Sewing machine
- ✳ Straight pins
- ✳ Iron and pad
- ✳ Pencil

1 Prepare the fabric. Press all the fat quarters to remove any folds and wrinkles. Trim each fat quarter and four pieces of flannel to 15″ (38cm) square.

2 Lay out the fabric. Form a stack of fabric for each placemat, placing the pieces in the following order from bottom to top: one square Fabric A right side up, one square Fabric B right side down, two squares flannel.

3 Mark the opening for turning. Make sure all four squares in each stack are smoothed out and the edges are flush, and then pin the pieces together. For each stack, mark a 5″ (12.5cm) space along the center of one of the edges, placing two pins on either side of the space. Skip over this 5″ (12.5cm) section when you sew the fabrics together. This will leave an opening for turning your placemat right side out after sewing.

⸙ TIP ⸙

The supplies listed will make two placemats.

Reversible Square Placemats *(continued)*

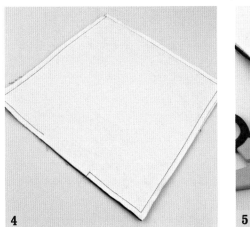

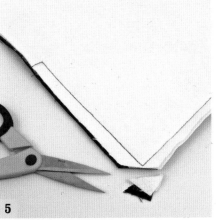

4 **Stitch the placemat.** Beginning at one end of the double-pinned space, stitch all the way around the perimeter of each stack using a ¼" (0.5cm) seam allowance. Remove the pins as you go. Stop when you reach the other end of the double-pinned space.

5 **Turn right side out.** Trim away a little fabric at the corners of each placemat to reduce bulk. Then, carefully turn them right side out through the opening left for turning. Use a knitting needle or a dull pencil to poke out the corners if necessary. Then press each placemat with a hot iron.

6 **Top stitch.** Starting at one corner, stitch all the way around the perimeter of each placemat, using a ⅜" (1cm) seam allowance. Tie off the thread ends on each side when finished.

⚜ TIPS ⚜

Pre-wash the fabrics and flannel in warm water on the gentle cycle to prevent shrinkage in the finished project.

These placemats can be put in the washer on the gentle cycle, line dried, and then pressed.

Two layers of flannel give each placemat enough thickness to lie flat without too much rigidity.

Use a walking foot on your sewing machine to prevent the fabrics from shifting as you sew.

Fabric Collage Wall Hanging

✿ **STASH ITEMS: Fabric scraps**

Foam panels wrapped with fabric make really pretty accents for home décor. Take it to the next level by making an artful collage of your favorite fabric scraps. I love to decorate the wall above the bed with foam panels because they're so lightweight...says the girl who lives in California earthquake country!

3 **4**

SUPPLIES
* 16" (40.5cm) square of solid color fabric
* Fabric scraps
* 12" (30.5cm) square smooth foam panel
* Liquid fabric glue
* Paintbrush
* Scissors
* Fabric shears
* Short straight pins
* Parchment paper
* Iron
* 11½" (29cm) square sheet of cardstock
* Small tag with reinforced hole
* Paper adhesive
* Fabric marker

1 **Prepare the fabrics.** Press all fabrics with an iron on high heat to remove folds and wrinkles.

2 **Prepare the foam.** Place parchment paper on top of the foam panel. Wrap the solid color fabric around the panel and pin it at the corners so your collage background area is clearly marked. The parchment paper will prevent the fabric from sticking to the foam if any glue seeps through.

3 **Prepare the pattern.** Scan the 7¼" (18.5cm) square flower pattern on page 87 and enlarge it 110%. Print it out tiled onto four sheets of paper. Cut out the shapes from the paper, and then pin and trace them onto scraps of fabric. Cut out each fabric shape with sharp fabric shears.

4 **Glue on the shapes.** Lay out each fabric shape on the background fabric where you want it. Then brush a light coat of fabric glue onto the back of each shape, bringing the glue all the way out to the edges, and press the shapes down into place on the background. Allow a few hours for the collage to dry.

Fabric Collage Wall Hanging (continued)

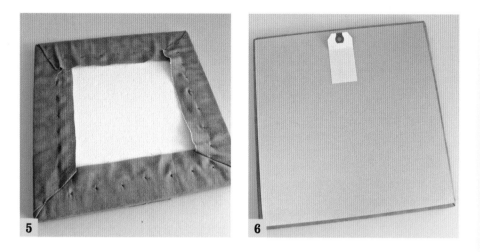

5 **Pin the background fabric.** Remove the collage from the foam to add decorative stitching if desired. Then reposition the fabric and wrap it around to the back of the foam. Miter the fabric at the corners like you're wrapping a present, and secure it with short pins. Push the pins into the foam at an angle so they don't poke through the front of the foam.

6 **Finish.** Glue a sheet of cardstock to the back of the foam to finish it off. Then adhere the bottom two-thirds of the tag near the top for hanging.

❦ TIPS ❧

After the glue is dry, but before pinning the collage to the foam panel, add some decorative stitching either by hand or machine. Be mindful of any glue residue that might make your needle a bit sticky—wipe the needle with some rubbing alcohol to clean it as needed.

Accent your collage by gluing on gems or buttons, or buy pressing short ball-head straight pins or colored thumbtacks into the foam through the fabric.

Instead of using my flower design, go rogue and create your own design or abstract arrangement. Let the colors and patterns of your fabric scraps guide you!

Fabric Collage Wall Hanging *(continued)*

Enlarge pattern 110% for actual size.

Index

Note: Page numbers in *italics* indicate projects.